Let's combine our sense of humour
And publish if we dare,
Some of our rhymes and musings
For other folk to share.
Let's do it now, before it's too late,
As friends have said we should,
And if we can make people smile,
Then that's all for the good.

A selection of rhymes written by
George Jackson and his daughter
Elizabeth Goodman (Nee Jackson).
Illustrated by Bruce Goodman.

First Published in Great Britain in 2012
by Green Square Books
www.greensquarebooks.com

A catalogue record for this book is available from the British Library.

ISBN 978-0-9573320-1-0

This book is printed using vegetable based inks and FSC (Forest Stewardship Council) certified paper. FSC-certified forests are managed in ways that safeguard long-term timber supplies, whilst protecting the environment and lives of forest-dependent peoples.

MIX
From responsible sources
FSC
www.fsc.org
FSC® C004411

green square
BOOKS

ELIZABETH GOODMAN
(Nee Jackson)

Dad

(Short and Sweet!)

You're always there when I need you,
Ready to help me if you can.
I've known you all my lifetime,
You're a very special man.

Though Mum's no longer with us,
And that sometimes makes me sad,
We still have you to care for us,
...I'm glad you are my Dad.

I'm a Rabbit.

I'm a rabbit, a creature of habit,
I sit in my hutch all the day.
Nose twitching, eyes blinking,
Who knows what I'm thinking,
As I while all the hours away.

I nibble on my greens,
And wonder what life means,
Why am I so incredibly sweet?
I think is it enough
To be a bundle of fluff,
With long fluffy ears and big feet.

Today just my luck, they passed me the buck,
But I was having none of it.
I'm sure he was foreign,
He was from another warren,
His name was Mervyn, a Welsh rarebit.

But I told him "NO". I'm not your doe/
"Hop it" I said, "Go elsewhere".
He didn't find it funny,
He was a Hot Cross Bunny,
And mad as a bloomin' March hare.

The thing is you see, motherhoods not for me,
I'd sooner just nibble on grass.
All that fornication,
And weeks of gestation
It's all one big pain in the A----

I'll let it be known,
I'm in a class of my own,
I'm not a rodent like a mouse or a rat.
I am of course , a Lagomorph,
And extremely proud of that.

In case you've not heard,
Of this technical word,
It means the teeth grow continuously,
And if the two sets don't meet,
They would grow several feet,
Which would be very unpleasant for me.

And for your information,
I perform pseudo rumination,
Which means I digest my food twice.
From your faces I see,
It's not your cup of tea,
But to a rabbit it tastes quite nice.

Did you hear about the bloke,
And this is no joke,
Whose scalp was incredible bare.
To make his ego feel big,
He wore a rabbit fur wig,
So from a distance it appeared he had hair.

There have indeed,
Been famous names among the breed.
The White Rabbit afraid of being late,
There was a rabbit who was friendly with Pooh,
Then there was Peter – he was great.

A farmer I guess, would consider me a pest,
If I nibbled on crops that he grew.
But he'll have no fun,
When he goes for his gun,
I for one won't end up in a stew.

'Cos I've got someone,
Who thinks she's my mum,
And she cares for me constantly.
So I say thanks very much,
For cleaning out my hutch,
Just how lucky can one rabbit be?

A Girl's Best Friend.

I've just split up with my boyfriend,
Though I don't really care.
I've got my eye on someone else,
Who's got more charm.........and hair.
I see him in the park each day,
Taking his daily walk.
I smile at him when he looks my way,
But never have the chance to talk.

He has the biggest brownest eyes,
That melt my heart away.
I wish for once he wouldn't pass me by
But turn, and sit, and stay.
I'm sure if he could understand,
Exactly how I feel,
He wouldn't want to run away,
He'd stay close at my heel.

I could learn to whistle,
Or to throw his favourite ball.
Just to be with him and have some fun,
I wouldn't mind at all.
I'd care for him and feed him well,
His trust I wouldn't fail.
I wouldn't ask much in return,
Just a lick, and a wag of his tail.

You may have guessed, he's not a man,
I can see you are all agog.
It's plain to see to anyone,
A girl's best friend is a DOG!

Keep Calm and Carry On.

I'll be glad when this war is over,
It's not safe for us girls left behind.
For the men left remaining,
Don't need entertaining,
They seem to have one thing on their minds.
Suddenly they all think they are Romeos,
And we should be glad they are there,
For while our boys are away,
The mice think they'll play,
And tread where the angels don't dare,

For instance, I went to the butchers,
And he said with a glint in his eye,
"If you play your cards right,
You could have steak tonight,
More than enough for a pie.
Come round the back of the shop,
I'll give you an extra pork chop,
Or maybe a nice bit of rump."
But I wouldn't risk it,
For that piece of old brisket,
Does he take me for some kind of chump?

And as I walked back from the Palais,
I heard a "Psst" in the alley.
I shouldn't have walked home on me own.
It was Harry the spiv,
He said "I know where you live,
I'll come round when your mother ain't home.
I've got some new nylons,
I want you to try on,
And French Knickers made of silk, trimmed with lace".
The cheeky young chap,
Well I gave him a slap,
That took the smile off his face,.

My friend Beryl can't decide,
Whether to become a war bride.
'Cos she's fallen in love with a Yank.
I said "Don't be silly,
You should hang on for your Willy,
Or Stanley, or Arthur, or Frank".
But she sighed - "But he's Randy",
And I bet he offered her candy,
We all know the point of his game.
She started to laugh,
"Oh, don't be daft,
Randy's not his mood – that's his name".

But then she's not that fussy,
She's a bit of a hussy,
Any old port in a storm.
Be it Tinker or Tailor,
Soldier or Sailor,
Her stair carpet's terribly worn.
I said "Be careful my dear,
For the walls have ears,
We should all be true sweethearts and wives,
And be careful what's said.
When the heart rules the head,
For careless talk costs lives".

And it's thanks to clothes rations,
I can't keep up with the fashions,
So I have to make do and mend.
Now I don't mind sharing,
But this dress that I'm wearing,
Belonged to a friend, of a friend, of a friend.
And the things Mum's been fixing,
Out there in the kitchen.
With what the coupons and rations allow,
Now I like me fried eggs,
But all we've got is dried eggs,
They don't taste the same somehow.

And dad's been digging for victory,
He's made a great hole in the yard.
His body was aching,
And his back it was breaking,
'Cos the ground was so blooming hard.
He said "I'll plant carrots, spuds and swedes,
That should supplement our needs,
As he supped on a beer for his thirst.
The fruits of his labour,
I'm sure we will savour,
If the dog don't dig 'em up first.

And as for that Herr Hitler,
He's a right little.............twit sir.
Him and his so-called master race,
Even our vicar, said he'd like to stick his swastika,
Up the opposite end to his face.
But when our boys return over,
The white cliffs of Dover,
We'll have street parties,
That's what we'll do.
For it will take more than some Sour Kraut,
To wipe us all out,
So three cheers for the Red, White and Blue!

The Sportsman.

My husband's taken up jogging,
In an effort to get fit.
He thinks he looks athletic,
I think he looks a TWIT!
He wears those skin-tight lycra shorts,
Showing all he's got.
He thinks he's Linford Christie,
I can assure you that he's not.

He thought he'd try his hand at squash,
He couldn't hit the ball.
The only thing that got squashed,
Was him against the wall.
So then he thought he'd try golf,
But he didn't get too far.
After three hours in a bunker,
He was certainly under par.

A mountain bike, his next idea,
Across the wild terrain.
With a fond farewell, and fingers crossed
I'd never see him again.
But thanks to the Mountain Rescue,
Far too clever at their job.
They managed to locate him,
...I should have slipped them a couple of bob.

I bought him a compendium of boardgames,
With those you are never too old.
Snakes and ladders gave him vertigo,
And with Draughts he caught a cold.
He got spots before his eyes with Dominoes,
A hopeless case you'd think.
At even the simplest of board games,
He couldn't get his tiddle to wink.

With a cricket bat he was lethal,
He swung it with such a clout.
With so much force he spun right round,
And knocked the umpire out.
Swimming was another thing,
He was such a stupid fool,
Diving in at the deep end,
...Well they should have filled the pool.

So now the failed sportsman,
Has finally reached his goal.
Flicking through the sports channels,
At the touch of the remote control.

A Fishy Tale.

I wish, I wish that I didn't stink of fish,
But I work on my Dad's fishmonger stall.
The aroma it lingers, and I've got fishy fingers,
It's not what I wanted at all.
People wouldn't turn up their noses if I smelt of roses,
I wish I worked in a perfumery.
Each night I'd go home, smelling of cologne,
Instead of something dredged up from the sea.

I'd swap a pint of mussels, for a pound of your Brussels,
I'd sooner work on the greengrocer's patch.
Selling nice juicy tomatoes, and King Edward potatoes,
Not this morning's fresh North Sea catch.
I gaze in despair at the fish lying there,
With glassy eyes staring into space.
Oh, if there's a God, take me away from this cod,
Oh please get me out of this place.

I've haddock and dabs – I'm sure I've got crabs,
And sprats that you fry in a pan.
I've halibut and trout, but be in no doubt,
I certainly ain't got no man!
Only if he were paid, could he love this mermaid,
Or if he had no sense of smell.
If my chests were much rounder, and not flat as a flounder,
I might stand a chance, who can tell?

I'd probably find a mate, down at old Billingsgate,
And his name would be Charlie or Reg.
And I bet for his tea, he'd want something fishy,
But I'd want me meat and two veg.
So please hear my plea, I'm not one for the sea,
I want the green fields of the countryside.
With a handsome young man, all bronzed and suntanned,
Not one who comes in – and goes out with the tide.

I bet sweet Molly Malone ended up on her own,
And she fared no better than me,
As she wheeled her wheelbarrow, through
streets broad and narrow,
And I bet she had kippers for tea.
I'm so full of woe, I can't stand cod roe,
Or soles that come from Dover.
I hate the feel of those jellied eels,
And cockles turn my stomach over.

I hope it's not too late, and it's not my fate,
To end up a fishmongers wife,
With a lobster-red face, guts all over the place,
Surrounded by fish all my life.
I might have hardships, and I've had my chips,
But I keep my hopes up to the end.
So don't say to me – worse things happen at sea,
I don't want to be a Fisherman's Friend!

Growing Pains.

Do you find as you grow older,
You remember things from the past.
It seems like only yesterday,
The years go by so fast.
I remember well the day I was born,
A wonderful experience for some.
But instead of the midwife smacking me,
She turned and smacked my mum.

Growing up was never easy,
I wore hand-me-down clothes from my brothers.
With baggy trousers and football boots,
… I stood out from all the others.
School was yet another trial,
Full of evil nasty creatures.
They used to tease and call me names,
And that was just the teachers.

So when it came to the school nativity play,
With a lazy eye, and teeth uneven and wonky.
No chance of me being the Virgin Mary,
So I was the back end of the donkey.
Another year, I hoped to be an angel,
But they made me a shepherd instead,
With one of Dad's old shirts tied at the waist,
And a tea towel wrapped round my head.

There were the school medicals, in the draughty school halls,
Because they cared for our welfare.
I queued with the rest, in my knickers and vest,
While the nit nurse dragged a comb through my hair.
She looked in my eyes, my ears and my throat,
She paused for a minute or two.
She checked my weight and my height – was I alright,
Then she sighed and she said "Oh, you'll do".

And when choosing teams for netball.
The captains picked their friends.
One by one they chose their sides,
... And there was me left at the end.
And the games we played in the playground,
I remember to this day,
Skipping, British Bulldog and Kiss Chase,
... And the boys all running away.

Teenage years – oh don't remind me,
With hormones changing all your bits.
And the extra hair you didn't want,
... And who invented zits?
There was always the classroom beauty,
Nice figure, nice hair teeth and br...chests.
Who was the first to wear a proper bra,
And there was me – still wearing a vest.

Once I went to the school disco,
Where I thought I might get a chance.
To show I was as "cool" as the other girls,
And a boy might even ask me to dance.
But come the last slow dance of the evening,
Nothing had gone as I planned.
And I danced all alone round me handbag,
With a bottle of coke in me hand.

I never mastered the art of make up,
Though I did as the beauty mags said.
But my efforts to, resemble a beauty model,
Looked like a monkeys bottom instead.
But then beauty is in the eye of the beholder,
It's only skin deep you see.
But that was no consolation,
There was still no-one looking at me!

But my mother told me not to worry,
And don't grow up too fast.
Perfect looks and perfect figures,
Are never going to last.
Just be yourself – and be proud,
You won't always be the classroom dunce.
I have to agree, she was right you see,
You'll all looking up to me for once.

Well I did finally meet a man and get married,
And I remember on my Wedding day
My Dad almost galloped me down the aisle,
Shouting "At last I'm giving her away".
So I didn't end up on the shelf,
Despite what the doubters had said.
And although I didn't have children,
I raised three rabbits instead.

I came into the world screaming and naked,
I shall probably go out the same way.
But though you may be the runt of the litter,
Remember, every dog has its day.
And so as I stand here before you,
Tomorrow you may not remember my name.
But you laughed with me – not at me,
And I've had my fifteen minutes of fame.

Moaner Liza.

Don't get me started on things that annoy me,
That vex me and give me the hump.
The tiniest things somehow,
Seem to bother me now,
And turn me into some kind of grump.
Like when you can't find the end of the sellotape,
Or undo the pickled onion jar,
Now I'm so hard to please,
Things I once did with ease,
All seem much harder than they are.

Why is there such rubbish on the telly,
What do I pay my licence fee for?
I've given up hope,
It's all football and soaps,
And repeats I've seen ten times before.
So I decided to go to the theatre,
For an evening of culture instead,
But the bloke in front of me,
Was as big as a tree,
And all I saw was the back of his head.

Why is my body going to pot,
Why do my knees and back ache?
I should be as fit as can be,
With all the Vitamin C,
And cod liver oil that I take.
Instead my bones are corroding,
My eyesights not good anymore.
A few teeth in the mouth,
And the boobs have gone south,
And hair grows where it didn't before.

I'd rather have piles than neighbours,
Both a pain in the rear to be sure.
For I expect some peace,
And the days troubles to cease.
When I am safe behind my closed door.
But there they go banging on the walls again,
Above the radio they make themselves known.
But I've told them before,
I'm not turning it up anymore.
They'll have to go and buy one of their own.

And if I should sit in the garden,
Enjoying the blue skies and sunshine.
Is there nothing more grimmer,
Than a Flymo or strimmer,
To shatter the peace that was mine.
And there's a dog constantly yapping,
Screaming kids in the garden behind,
Then someone decides to
Have a stinking Bar-b-Q,
How's a person supposed to unwind.

And if that football comes over the hedge one more time,
I'll spear it with my garden fork.
There's no truer word,
Children should be seen not heard.
Curse the gooseberry bush – and the stork,
Tell me why does the neighbours cat,
Prefer my garden instead of its own.
Now my newly planted flower bed,
Looks like a bombsite instead,
With the special "presents" that kitty has sown.

So why when I've hung out the washing,
Does it suddenly pour down with rain.
I can't seem to win,
'Cos when I bring it back in,
In five minutes the sun's out again.
And the bird sitting in the tree singing,
With his melodic song and trill calls.
When my back is turned,
I know I'll be spurned,
And he'll mess all over me smalls.

Seems like everything is against me,
Can't something nice happen instead.
Why with sleep in my eyes,
As I stumble to rise,
Do I stub my toe on the edge of the bed.
And the toast that I made for breakfast,
Lands butter-side down on the floor.
And when I'm sat on the loo,
As we're all prone to do,
Someone decides to knock at the door.

Don't phone me when I am busy,
Or just pop round for a bit of a chat.
Let's not meet for lunch,
Coffee – or brunch,
I can't be doing with that.
And don't ask me to come to your parties,
I'm perfectly happy on my own.
What's my excuse?
I've become a recluse,
I vant to be left alone.

Cruising.

A lonely disheartened spinster,
I decided to banish the blues.
With the promise of sun, sea and good fun,
I booked myself up on a cruise.
There may be a chance,
Of a shipboard romance,
With someone in the same boat as me.
Oh it would be grand,
To stroll hand in hand,
Round the decks looking far out to sea.

I went to the afternoon tea dance,
It was pleasant enough …just.
There was no sign of man,
So me and this woman called Ann,
Waltzed and tangoed together bust to bust.
Later at the Captain's Gala Dinner,
Dressed in me posh frock and pearls,
I caught the eye,
Of a handsome young guy,
He said I stood out from the rest of the girls.

I blushed, was it my pearly white teeth
Or my perfect skin without any flaws.
He said "I noticed when you,
Came back from the loo,
Your dress was tucked up in your drawers".
Filled with shame and embarrassment,
I took myself off to the bar.
So much for a holiday romance,
I hadn't had much luck so far.

The wine was flowing like water,
And I acted like such a fool.
For I hardly drink any,
But I had one too many,
And promptly fell off me stool.
I awoke in a strange white room,
I thought I'd died and gone to Heaven.
I looked up into the eyes of the ship's doctor,
He looked just like "007".

So I did my best impression of Mae West,
And said "Come up and see me sometime".
"There's no need" he said,
"It's just a bump on the head,
In a couple of days you'll be fine".
So here I am, still free and single,
Still sleeping alone in my bed,
Next year wait and see,
No more cruisin' for me,
I think I'll go fishing instead.

Shotgun Wedding.

I'm having to get married,
A shotgun wedding you might say.
Because I had some fun, with a farmers son,
In the stables, in the hay.

Well I didn't know what was happening,
I hadn't got a clue.
Being so sweet and innocent,
I didn't know what to do.

Ah, but now my dreams are over,
I could have been a star,
With a big posh house and swimming pool,
And a shiny, flashy car.

Instead I'll be a farmers wife,
Strong and hearty and fit.
With a farmyard full of children,
On a tractor I shall sit.

Mum's gone out and bought a hat,
And Dad's brushed down his suit.
He's been searching in the cupboards,
For the Brylcreem and the Brut.

We're having the reception,
Down at the village hall.
Nothing grand you understand,
We want to keep it small.

I've borrowed this dress from my cousin,
Because she is rather plump.
Well I had to get a bigger size,
To try and hide "THE BUMP!"

My Fiance now will have to change his ways,
No more fun and fancy-free.
Just like his horse, he's had his oats,
And now he's stuck with me.

And so I'm standing here outside the Church,
Flashing a cheesy grin.
I expect I'll be back in a few month's time,
... for the Christening.

The Downtrodden Wife.

For years I've been a farmers wife,
But all was not as it seems.
For once we were wed,
I found out instead,
He wasn't the man of my dreams.
While we were courting, life was so sweet,
I couldn't wish for a nicer fella.
But once over the threshold,
His loving went cold,
And he treated me like Cinderella.

"Fetch my food wife, polish my boots",
He yelled at the top of his voice.
Cooking and cleaning,
Life had no meaning,
He wasn't this housewife's choice.
"Iron my shirt, fetch me my cap,
Darn my sock, there's a dirty great hole".
And at night by the fire,
As I started to tire,
"WOMAN! Go fetch some more coal".

In all kinds of weather you'd find me,
Chasing livestock all over the place.
He had me driving a tractor,
No time for Max Factor.
With mud and muck stuck all over me face,
So I made him his favourite currant cake,
And told him I didn't care for it much.
I started to snigger,
And said "I'm watching me figure",
... Thanks for the rabbits in their hutch!

Young girls take heed of my warning,
Don't fall for the boys in the field.
For it's not carrots and onions,
But callouses and bunions,
That will be the harvest you yield.
I bore him a couple of children,
Not out of love...........more a whim,
My bundles of joy,

Two big bouncing boys,

... who looked exactly like him!

Through being his wife, I've ruined my life,
And I'm still only aged forty three.
Still he's cooked his goose now,
He can go marry a cow.
And I hope she'll be happier than me!
But no more of my complaining,
I see a new future in sight,
For as my old man sleeps,
An appointment I'll keep,
I'm running off with the milkman tonight.

My Little Rant.

I may not be a genius,
And know the ins and outs of it all.
But don't treat me like an idiot,
Or nothing more than a fool.
I know when I'm being patronised,
I know when I'm being praised,
I can normally rise above things,
I don't get too easily "phased".
Just remember we both started the same way,
Naked and screaming at birth,
We'll both go out the same way.
With nothing of value or worth.

You can't take anything with you,
Whether you've acquired fortune or fame.
Some will remember you fondly,
Others will curse at your name.
The posh house and the smart car are nothing,
They are just material things.
They cannot compare to simple pleasures,
And the joy true happiness brings.
So don't judge me on appearances,
Or the type of job I do.
I have no airs and graces,
But I'm far better off than you!

"Bah Humbug!"

I'll be glad when this Christmas is over,
And the plastic tree is back in its box.
And I'll make room once more,
In my bottom drawer,
For the unwanted hankies and socks.
And the jumper that Aunty Dora knitted,
I'll make certain nobody sees.
In stripes green and white,
With a neckband too tight,
And sleeves that come down to my knees!

I'll be glad when the eating is over,
We've had turkey, cold, curried and hot.
I've been up to my eyes,
In sausage rolls and mince pies,
And enough sprouts to fill the sails of a yacht.
We've nibbled on dates, figs and peanuts,
And the Christmas cake has lasted a week.
And the trifle laced with sherry,
Made Aunty Flo merry,
And she kissed Uncle Fred on the cheek.

I'll be glad when the drinking is over,
I've had too much sherry and wine.
My old man's full of cheer,
'Cos he's drunk so much beer,
And his nose is starting to shine.
The kids are bored with their presents already,
There's nothing much on the TV,
I'm far too knackered,
To pull one more cracker,
And the fairy has fallen off the tree.

I'll be glad when the partyings over,
And we've played all the board games,
Monopoly and Trivial Pursuit,
Always end in dispute,
And calling each other names.
Let me get rid of this silly paper hat,
And relax in my comfy armchair,
And pass me that box,
Of fattening milk chocs,

Its Christmas, so I don't bloomin' care!
I'll be glad to take down the decorations,
And wait for the last guest to leave,
For I can't be jolly,
With my hall decked with holly,
'Cos I know they'll be back New Years Eve.
Then there will be more eating and drinking,
As we wait for the chimes of Big Ben,
And fuelled with whisky and wine,
We'll sing Auld Lang Syne,
And next year we'll do it all again.

I'll be glad when the snow has all melted,
You can keep your Christmas of white.
I cringe when I hear Bing,
And the choir start to sing,
How I long for a Silent Night.
So I'll be glad when Christmas is over,
And all the preparations that it entails,
Now my time can be spent,
Buying next year's presents,
For half price in the January sales!

Stagestruck.

Oh give me a chance,
To sing and to dance.
My dream from a very young age,
With my repertoire,
I'm sure I'll go far,
I was born to be on the stage.

I could be Singing in the Rain,
Or maybe Calamity Jane,
I can be down to earth or aloof,
And I bet at a pinch,
If I'm given an inch,
I'm sure I could Fiddle on the Roof.

Oh it would be terrific,
To star in South Pacific,
I close my eyes and imagine I'm there.
And across the blue sea,
Bali Hai would call me,
And I'd Wash that man out of my Hair.

I'll do my magic,
Be it comic or tragic,
As I wait for my cue in the wings.
Oh it would be nice,
To sing Edelweiss,
And list All my favourite Things.

They may not all clap,
When I start to tap.
For believe me it's harder than you think,
When I hear the chords,
And jump up on "The Boards",
I usually end up in the sink.

But you'll all know my name,
When I achieve fame,
There'll be a star on my dressing room.
I'll be all the rage,
When I sweep the stage
With my talent, not the end of a broom.

But you wait and see,
Nothing will change me,
With all the glamour and glitz of showbiz.
Though I may be showered,
With champagne and flowers,
I will still always be just "Liz".

LONESOME TONIGHT
(With apologies to Elvis).

You'll be lonesome tonight,
'Cos you give him a fright,
Every time you walk through the door.
And though it's hard to say,
I'm afraid you must pay
My dear, He don't love you no more.
If you put back the glass eye,
And keep the teeth in,
Then there may be a chance,
That his love you could win.
But the state of you now,
Turns his stomach somehow,
That is why dear, you'll be lonesome tonight.

You'll be lonesome tonight,
And I know it's not right,
You probably can't help it at all.
But your hair is a wig,
And your bum is too big,
Either that our your drawers are too small.
Where is the young girl,
That he doted on,
Your get up and go dear,
Has got up and gone.
Now you make him feel sick,
You smell of garlic and Vick,
That is why dear
You'll be lonesome tonight.

You'll be lonesome tonight,
And it gives him delight,
To tell you he's leaving today.
Now he's all set to roam,
Even the dog has left home,
And you've scared all the neighbours away.
He no longer wants you,
To share his warm bed,
For he's found another
And his name is FRED.
Though it pains me to say,
You have made him turn gay,
That is why dear,
You'll be lonesome tonight.

It's Over.

My husband's going to leave me soon,
For someone else I fear.
He doesn't cuddle me no more.
Or kiss, or call me DEAR.
I wish I knew the reason why,
His love has gone astray.
Or what it is that I have done,
To make him turn away.

Could it be I've lost my charm,
For when we go off to bed
And I am feeling "IN THE MOOD",
He reads a book instead.
Maybe the see-through negligee,
Doesn't thrill him anymore,
Or is it because I lay on my back
And snore, and snore, and snore!

Perhaps if I took the curlers out,
And kept the false teeth in.
And wore a touch of make-up,
His attention I could win.
And if I pulled my stockings up,
And my clothes were not so tatty,
I might look more like Zsa Zsa Gabor
Instead of Norah Batty.

He's using lots of aftershave,
He never did before.
And combs his hair at least three times,
Before he leaves the door.
He says that he is going to see,
A man about a dog.
He comes home way past midnight,
When I'm sleeping like a log.

Well last night he dropped a bombshell,
As he walked through the door.
He said "My dear it's over,
I don't love you anymore".
He said if I was lucky,
I could find another man.
And then he introduced me,
To his new partner .... STAN!

So now I'm worried,
It's flot a phase he's going through.
His'mid-life crisis,
Is making me feel blue.
He's been straying, like a smelly tomcat,
So I'm going back to Mother,
'Cos he's run off with another,
But I never thought he'd do that!

Bargains.

I can't resist a bargain,
So I bought one, and got one free.
But "Super Ramrod" aftershave,
Is not much use to me.

I got fifty per cent extra free,
And I was very pleased with that.
On chicken and rabbit cat food,
… But I haven't got a cat!

A bumper pack of curries,
A bit excessive, you might have thought.
But they made good use, I'll have you know,
Of the king-size loo rolls that I bought.

The beans I bought, a pack of six,
I ate one can a day.
The aftermath, I must confess,
Kept all my friends away.

The dress I got, with ten pounds off,
Though it doesn't really fit.
Unless I lose a stone or two,
And breathe in quite a bit.

A lovely pair of leather shoes,
A snip at fifteen pounds.
They really don't hurt all that much,
If I curl my big toes round.

I've queued for hours outside the stores,
Waiting for the sales to start.
With thermos flask and sleeping bag,
Praying for the doors to part.

Boot sales, Jumble or Table Top,
Where there are bargains to be found.
I'll haggle 'til I'm blue in the face,
But I'll never spend more than a pound.

Spinsters Lament.

Oh when will somebody love me?
When will I find my man?
Someone to hold and caress me,
And take me by the hand.

When will I hear the violins?
As he thrills me with his kiss.
Will I ever walk down the aisle,
Must I always be a Miss?

Must I always buy frozen meals for one,
At the supermarket store?
Where's the dark handsome stranger,
Who will knock upon my door?

Must it always be the milkman,
Who looks like Benny Hill.
Why is it always the postman,
Bringing another bill.

Oh whisk me away from this drudgery,
Don't leave me on the shelf.
I'm tired of sleeping all alone,
... and talking to myself.

My mother said "Never trust a man,
He'll lead you a merry dance".
Well I know it takes two to tango,
... But I've never had the chance.

There must be someone out there,
Who'll take me for what I am.
A frustrated, disillusioned spinster,
... who's desperate for a MAN.

GEORGE C JACKSON OF WALTON-ON-THE-NAZE

A collection of my thoughts I've
written down in rhyme.

Please sit down and read them,

If you can spare the time,

The Garden

Published in a national garden circular.

It's good to have a garden in which to spend the hours,
Producing nice fresh vegetables, or maybe pretty flowers.
When you dig, hoe or weed, doing things at leisure.
Take time to look around you, it all adds to the pleasure.

The bees and butterflies come to the flowers, to feed on nectar sweet,
While the birds will gather round, the grubs and worms to eat.
The summer brings the swallows to disperse the flies,
Which seem to gather round you and get into your eyes.

The vegetables that you produce, do in point of fact,
Have a better flavour than the ones you buy pre-packed.
Fresh flowers from the garden, anyone can tell,
Were not bought at the florists, they have a sweeter smell.

It might be more convenient to purchase items from the shop,
But the gardener who works sensibly, and does not go non-stop,
Can benefit enormously in fitness and healthwise,
If he goes into the garden for fresh air and exercise.

A Corny Tale.

A grumpy farmer, name of Street,
Used the word corn, instead of wheat.
When at breakfast one wet morn,
Said "The rain's playing havoc with my corn"
Bemoaning the fact to his dear wife,
Who'd borne his complaints all their married life.
Herself being troubled with painful feet,
Decided she'd give themselves a treat.
So telling him "Not to worry Dear,
I'll get somebody to call here"
Then taking the telephone off the hook,
A chiropodist's services she did book.
Later that day there appeared a fella ,
Under one arm he carried an umbrella.
As he stood outside the byre,
Short and fat, with a large spare tyre
Hanging over his trouser belt,
A distinct cold atmosphere was felt.
The farmer glared at his wife, and said,
"You've got a screw loose in your head,
How much of my crop do you think he'll shield,
If he holds that thing up in my field?"

Dave the Barber.

We have a local barber, his name is David Benn.
And once you've been inside his shop, you'll surely go again.
The shop it may be crowded, have a coffee while you wait
Until you're in the chair and Dave attacks your pate.

The more the people in the shop, of topics there's no limit,
And the floor gets covered with tufts of hair
as Dave with flair will trim it.
Your hair may hang down shoulder length or halfway to your knees,
But if you've hardly any, Dave charges you search fees.

You may hear a story that might make you laugh,
Don't do it when you're in the chair,
Dave might cut your ear in half.
Sometimes a lad might sneak in, a five pound note to spend,
It makes you think, when with a wink, Dave says "Have a good weekend".

So if you're in the neighbourhood and have some time to spare,
Call in, you're always welcome if you can find a chair.

PICKLE

A young man went to work one day in a terrible huff,
He said to his mate, "I'm in a state, my girlfriend can't get enough.
I'm young and strong, but won't be for long,
As she goes into a fit,
And stamps on the floor, then asks for more,
Demanding that I give her it.
With luck I am able, if I stand on the table,
To reach up to her top shelf,
And then I stand with it in my hand,
And say here it is, help yourself.
With eyes open wide, she pops it inside.
As I look at her distended belly,
I visibly quake, my knees start to shake,
And my legs go wobbly like jelly.
I'm all for some slap and tickle,
But I get no delight, last thing at night,
To see her scoff down a jarful of pickle".

The Nudist.

On the nudist beach one day, a man was seen to show,
A worried expression as his gaze swept to and fro.
Though rather short in stature this unlucky gent,
As a result of overeating was very corpulent.
It seems, he took his young son to the beach, held firmly by the hand,
Then went to get some ices, while the lad played in the sand.
On returning to the spot where he had left his chair,
Somehow he couldn't see the young lad sitting there.
The man called to a lady nearby, and said "This may sound silly,
I know where he should be, but I can't see my willy".
The woman said "You stupid man, you must think me green,
Your willy's in the place where it has always been".

Based on a Saucy Seaside Postcard.

Two overworked East End housewives had as much as they could take,
So decided together they'd take a well-earned break.
And leave the kids behind them, and simply idle on the sand,
To recharge their batteries, in a far off distant land.
On a beach that was deserted except for passing shipping,
They even had some time to indulge in skinny-dipping.
When one looked out to sea one day,
A smile came to her face.
A sight looked so familiar, albeit out of place.
Way out on the water, beyond a passing sail,
Was the outline of an island, which looked so like a male,
Lying in the water, undressed. Apart from socks.
On it stood a lighthouse, with seaweed round its rocks.
As she gave her friend a nudge, she said,
"Hey Gert.
What does that remind you of? It reminds me of my Bert!"

MEN'S CLUB STORY.

A lady golfer on the links was practising one day,
When she gave a ball a hefty hit and it sailed off far away.
A groundsman on another green, his mind set on his task,
Was hit by the speeding ball, where you need not ask.
His immediate reaction was to give a mighty yell.
"Your blasted ball just hit me, and it hurts like hell!"

When she came up to him, as he rolled beneath the trees,
She saw he had his legs crossed, and his hands between his knees.
"I'm a professional lady", fainting, he heard her say,
"Perhaps you would feel better if I rubbed the pain away".
What she then done to him, took him by surprise,
But he laid back and enjoyed it as he watched with half-closed eyes.

When she asked if that felt better, he said "It's my belief,
That was not the first time you've given hand relief.
But to be quite honest, it still feels rather numb,
That wasn't where you hit me, you hit me on the THUMB".

Pot Luck.

An explorer in the jungle, thought he was on a winner,
When he met a pygmy, who invited him to dinner.
His hungry mouth was watering as they set off down a trail,
How soon would he stave his hunger? On what feast would they regale?

As they reached a clearing, what a shock he got,
When he realised that he was destined for the pot.
White with fear he pleaded "Spare my life I beg",
"OK" said the pygmy, "But it'll cost you an arm and leg".

The man refused to bargain, and got hit on the head.
Then ended up with all of him in the pot instead.
The pygmy then sat down to eat, 'til he could scoff no more,
And then he crumpled in a heap and exploded on the floor.
Looking at his burst stomach, said "It's plain to see
I should not have eaten someone who disagreed with me".

The moral of this story, neither would have died,
If they had chewed it over and just swallowed their pride.
The explorer with his mobile (even in the scrub)
Could have called up for assistance and a supply of grub.

Neighbours.

A kind man used to help a neighbour with her chores,
While she dealt with those inside the house he dealt with those outdoors.
She appreciated what he did, and thought he was a treasure,
While he was happy to oblige as it gave him lots of pleasure.
She rewarded him with a meal sometimes, or a small amount of cash,
For no matter what the task, he always had a bash.
It was unfortunate he was simple in the head,
And didn't always understand what to him was said.
It happened as he worked shirtless, one hot summer morn,
She in a bikini gaily mowed the lawn.
Later sitting on the grass, having a cooling drink,
She looked across at him and gave a crafty wink.
Then said "I haven't any money so I wonder if you'd mind,
If I rewarded you with payment of another kind".
He replied, "I cycle to see the barmaid at the Jolly Rover,
But of late I've had a problem getting my leg over.
However I accept your offer, what I would really like,
As it hasn't got a crossbar, can I have your bike?"

ANGLERS.

From experience.

Anglers come from far and near,
And dangle their worms on the local pier.
Some are content to sit for hours,
Regardless of the sun or showers.
With a gutful of spirits I've been told,
They don't even feel the cold.

You find some amidst the eager punters,
The ones they call "The Bounty Hunters",
Who enter all the competitions,
And pray for yearly repetitions,
To win the top prize and the cash,
Which makes it worthwhile to have a bash.

Some you find, the other sort,
Who do it simply for the sport.
Or who do prefer a quiet life,
Away from yelling kids and wife.
And wish for all the world they can,
Catch a fish for the frying pan.

There are those who meet together,
For club comps, despite the weather.
One questions, "Are they past their prime?"
Or do they simply pass the the time,
On the pier or in the pub,
Why are so few ladies in the club?

WALTON-ON-THE-NAZE.

I live in a seaside town called Walton-on-the-Naze,
But being on the North Sea coast, we get some windy days.
Strangers to the town strolling on the prom,
Sometimes get blown back to where they started from.

Anglers on the pier (this is not a fisherman's tale)
Have been known to lose a big fish when it blows off in a gale.
And as other anglers laugh at them. Adding to their troubles,
They watch it swim away, leaving a trail of bubbles.

If a reveller has too much to drink, followed by a curry snack,
He checks the way the wind blows, lest he gets his own back.
I'm not bothered by the wind so I don't give two hoots,
Having lived here several years, I have well-established roots.

But a word of advice to someone coming here on holiday,
Take out a large insurance, you might get blown away.
Make sure it is a good one, the best you can afford,
In case when you come down to earth, you may be far abroad.

My Pets by Miss. Inga Lott (missing a lot).

I always longed to have a pet, since I was just a child.
But my parents blunt refusal used to make me wild.
As years passed by and I left home, I thought I'd take the chance
To keep a pet (a few in fact) but they led me quite a dance.

The first I had (a little dear) a fluffy tabby kitten
Who'd play with me the whole day through, I was really smitten.
The crunch came when I went out to work, the outcome you can guess.
When I came home one evening and found an awful mess.
The flower vase on the carpet and water on the floor
And a heap I put my foot in as I walked through the door.

My second was a bunny, with long and floppy ears
I had him quite a long while, it must have been five years.
I loved my little bunny, I used to call him Shaun
He would hop and skip with me, as we frolicked on the lawn.
He looked so cute and lovable as I stroked him on my knee,
But when I put him on the ground, he bucked and squirted me.
I couldn't cure my bunny of this unpleasant habit
And so it was I said goodbye to Shaun my lovely rabbit.

My third, a dog I really liked, with brown and dreamy eyes
But he'd see any other off, regardless of their size.
He loved to go for walkies and round the park we'd pound.
The problem was he always went with his nose glued to the ground.
He hadn't another habit with didn't really please,
He always pulled me off the path, so he could kick the trees.

I kept a little pot-bellied pig, so cute when he was small,
But he grew up to be a size and nearly blocked the hall.
He grew fat on scraps from mealtimes and pellets meant for goats,
But squealed and grunted loudly, 'cos he couldn't get his oats.
Then when he'd finished feeding, he'd rock the house with snores.
I couldn't stand it any longer and put him out of doors.
In time I wish that I'd kept my snappy little dog,
He did have better manners than my disgusting hog.

My next pet was a budgie in a lovely ornate cage,
The pretty bird was company and blue was all the rage.
For hours I'd sit beside him and try to make him talk,
But it was all time wasted, he wouldn't even squawk.
When my patience was exhausted and I sat down in my chair,
He'd sit behind me in his cage and gently tweak my hair.
And then quite unexpectedly this stupid bird,
Would flutter wildly round his cage and cover me with feathers, husk and turd.

Of pets I was despairing, when I thought what I could do.
I could adopt an inmate at the local zoo.
I couldn't make my mind up when the choice I had to make,
A bird, a carnivore or primate, or perhaps a snake.
A little greenback monkey, the choice I finally made
And so the annual adoption fee was duly paid.
One day I paid a visit, mainly just to see
How my pet was faring, and if he remembered me.
I was amazed to see his friends all paired up on the shelf
While he was in a corner, playing with himself.

Now I'm approaching middle age and haven't got a pet
But there is one I fancy so I may get one yet.
It belongs to my neighbour and if I'm very quick,
I can see it through the curtain perform its favourite trick.
Now I know what fun I'm missing I'll get one when I can.
It's what I've always wanted, a hunky virile man.

Darby and Joan.

Darby, an Irishman tired of living on his own,
So he joined a folk dance club, to maybe meet a Joan.
A friend said if he joined, the chances then,
Were that the ladies present far outnumbered the men.
And if he learned some basic steps, perchance,
He could become a favourite partner for a dance.
The first lady that he danced with, all flashing eyes and teeth,
Although she had hot hands, was frigid underneath.
Another caught his eye as across the floor she flounced,
He was fascinated by the way her ample bosom bounced.
She said she'd been an actress to whom the audience would warm,
Though now up in her eighties, she could still perform.
Poor Darby thought that he could handle all her blubber,
But was put off by the fact, she had also been a scrubber.
He then eyed up another who looked good enough to eat,
And the chat up line he used seemed to work a treat.
Though she was plastered up with make-up and looking quite a sight,
He could feel it in his water with her he'd be all right.
After a few weeks, they were getting on so well,
That he wined and dined her at a posh hotel.
Sitting at the table it came as a surprise,
She didn't seem to mind as he slyly stroked her thighs.
Later, on the back seat of a taxi cab,
He went a bit further and made a crafty grab.
Then he made a discovery, about which he dare not brag,
He had wasted time and money on a fellow dressed in drag.

The Wages of SIN.

A vicar went to London on an annual seminar
Got lost, ran out of petrol, so he had to leave his car.
Despite having a map, and directions written down,
He discovered that he was in the red light part of town.

Going to a cafe, through the window he was able,
To see a stunning redhead seated at a table.
Rolling up his scarf, so his collar wasn't shown,
He went inside and asked if she was eating on her own.

When she said "As yet I am" he sat down, and slyly
Introduced himself as Mr. Michael Riley.
Then he boldly asked, if she thought he might
Take him to her home, where he could spend the night.

Then off they went together, he was amazed to see,
The magnificent apartment where she lived in luxury.
When the morning came she said, "My fees 100 nicker"
He said "I cannot pay it, I am a poorly paid town vicar".

"But now I've thought about it, the Church I'll have to quit,
There's more money in your business, and I'd like a bit of it".
So he went and sold his car, then took out a bank loan,
To buy a massage parlour and set up on his own.

He then got a host of good-time girls that he kept within
Now he lived the life of Riley, on the wages of sin.
And drinks and feasts on everything he couldn't once afford,
When he was just a vicar singing praises to the LORD.

The Escape.

In the prison gym, two convicts worked hard to get in shape,
As together they planned to make good their escape.
Theirs was a simple plan – they would create a riot,
And in the ensuing confusion was the the time that they would try it.
At a given signal, things went to their plans,
Everything got smashed up including toilet pans.
At a press conference later, a spokesman from the Met,
Said "There was nothing for his men to go on yet.
What would really help us in our hour of need,
Is a scent for our dog to follow, but we haven't got a lead"
Meanwhile the two escapees somewhere along the road,
Had hijacked a lorry and feasted on its load.
Unfortunately for them, these two stupid goons,
Didn't realise what happens, when you eat too many prunes.
In the follow-up procedure, which was duly done,
The police were now looking for two men "on the run".
Local farmers joined in the hunt as a result of which,
The men were apprehended squatting in a ditch.
At a later hearing the judge was seen to frown,
At the superintendents remark "caught with their trousers down".

The Suffolk Punch.

Published in the Suffolk Punch Monthly letter.

The Suffolk Punch, a grand old horse, a breed of great distinction,
Now has a place in history and faces near extinction.
What brought about this happening, there is one major factor,
Three pairs working on a field, could not out-pace one tractor.

Small farmers with small fields, enclosed with five-barred gates,
Were taken on by syndicates and formed into large estates.
Field boundaries were extended, which brought about of course,
An area far greater to be managed by the horse.

The hours of daylight ruled the time when horses worked (quite right)
But sitting in a tractor cab, a man works half the night.
Four pairs of punches and four men, were sometimes to be found,
Now one man on a tractor speeds across the ground.

Four feet worked in unison, each one nicely spread.
And far less soil compaction than the tractors mighty tread.
The tractor draws many furrows, plus a roll and harrow,
While a pair of punches could only make make one farrow

To be economical, lost time was money lost,
So men opted for the tractor, regardless of the cost.
Though the horses days were numbered, it is not too late,
To try to save the breed who face the dodo's fate.
By all means use a tractor 'til it's no use because,
Man can make another tractor, but can't produce a horse.

A Moment of Reverie.

As you climb the mountain of lifetimes winding stair,

You can't see round the corner, when you think you're halfway there.

Ponder for a moment, and I think you'll find,

As many steps before you as you have left behind.

When you reach the summit, do as I will do,

Reflect on your achievements, and enjoy the view.

Acknowledgements to

Bruce Goodman (son in law and husband)
for the illustrations

Christine Bright (eldest daughter and sister)
for typing out the poems originally

Alison Ovenden (youngest daughter and sister)
for the photo of Dad and I

All friends and family who have encouraged us
to pursue this venture.

I was born in October 1957 the middle one of three daughters of Eunice and George Jackson. I lived for the first 3 years in a farm cottage as dad worked on a local farm in Kirby-le-Soken, where he was born and raised.

In 1960 we moved to Walton-on-the-Naze, where mum was born and raised as dad got a new job with a local building firm and needed extra money to pay for his family.

I attended the local primary and junior school and mostly remember the endless long summer holidays and spending the whole day down the beach with my cousins at our nanna's beach hut. When I was 14 I had a summer job waitressing in a fish and chip shop style restaurant, the perks were a free dinner every day but the downside was constantly smelling of fish and chip fat!

Failing my 11 Plus I went to Gunfleet Secondary Modern (as it was named then) and left in 1974 aged 16½ armed with 7 CSE's and 1 O Level in Art. A week later I started working in a local silk screen printing firm, where I met Bruce my future husband. One of the first things he said to me was that he was never going to get married, but 11 years later we got married on my 28th Birthday. We set up home in Colchester as it was nearer to the jobs we had at the time.

Around 1995 I joined a local variety group inspired by my sister Alison who was already a member. We would put on little shows for local clubs in the area in village halls. This is how I came to start writing monologues and performing them. The group disbanded but Alison and I went on to join the local group we are currently at called The Haven Lights, based in Holland-on-Sea. Since being with The Haven Lights I have also appeared as a solo act as part of the Mother's Day Musical Shows put on by the Young Brothers at the Westcliff Theatre in Clacton.

I think I inherited my artistic flair from my mother ands my sense of humour and wit form dad. Sadly mum died in 1998 aged just 63 and she is very much still missed by all of us.

I decided against motherhood myself and opted for pet rabbits instead! As for the collection of peoms, dad and I have often been told we should publish them so the time seems right, and while we are both still alive and kicking we are doing as we've been told.

Hope you enjoy,

Elizabeth Goodman

I was born on 9th October 1930 at Kirby le Soken, one of 4 children - I had 2 sisters and 1 brother. In 1940 as a result of a threat of a German invasion during WW2, my elder brother myself and the oldest of my younger sisters were evacuated to Gloucester, from June until December. With school being closed primary education took place in private houses a few hours a week. At 11 years old, I resumed at Walton on the Naze Secondary School. I left school at 14 years old and went to work as a boy on a builders pay roll, being paid £1.00 per week. At 16 years old I went to work on a farm, in the milking sheds. After getting married in 1954 I was granted a farm cottage; my wage was 3 pounds and 15 shillings after a small amount was taken for our rent. Two daughters were born and a third expected when I left my job and took out a mortgage on a terraced property in Walton, also getting employment with a local builder, decorator and undertaker. Having a good employer I was encouraged to pick up a trade and become quite useful with a trowel, carrying out bricklaying, drainage, plastering, tiling and decorating - working on a fair number of kitchens, bathrooms extensions in the area. I remained loyal to my employer until I retired at 65 years of age, after 35 years in the firm's employ - I would have stayed longer but I had been in full employment since I left school in 1944, a total of 51 years.

My biggest regret I was unable to spend more of my retirement years with my wife Eunice, who as a result of a serious lung condition passed away aged 63 in March 1998, whilst at The Royal Brompton Hospital in Chelsea.

George Jackson